SUPER LANDS

Consultant : Peter B. Stifel
Illustrators: Barbara Gibson, Stuart Armstrong

Published by
The National Geographic Society
John M. Fahey, Jr., President and Chief Executive Officer
Gilbert M. Grosvenor, Chairman of the Board
Nina D. Hoffman, Senior Vice President
William R. Gray, Vice President and Director, Book Division

Staff for this Book
Barbara Brownell, Director of Continuities
Marianne R. Koszorus, Senior Art Director
Toni Eugene, Editor
Alexandra Littlehales, Art Director
Catherine Herbert Howell, Writer-Researcher
Susan V. Kelly, Illustrations Editor
Sharon Kocsis Berry, Illustrations Assistant
Mark A. Caraluzzi, Director of Direct Response Marketing
Heidi Vincent, Product Manager
Vincent P. Ryan, Manufacturing Manager
Lewis R. Bassford, Production Project Manager

Visit our Web site at www.nationalgeographic.com

Library of Congress Catalog Card Number: 00-133630
ISBN: 0-7922-3461-8

Color separations by Quad Graphics, Martinsburg, West Virginia
Printed in Mexico by R.R. Donnelley & Sons Company

SUPER LANDS

Catherine Herbert Howell

NATIONAL
GEOGRAPHIC
SOCIETY

INTRODUCTION

North America is a continent full of super lands. Super lands are landforms, or features of the Earth's surface, that are among the biggest, most unusual, and most spectacular features in the world. Landforms include mountains, plains, canyons, and even islands. This book also includes water features in North America such as rivers, lakes, and waterfalls.

Some super lands are created by forces within the Earth. The surface of the Earth is made up of huge slabs of rock called plates. When they move, they can create mountains, volcanoes, and deep cracks on the Earth's surface, such as the San Andreas Fault. Water, wind, and ice weather, or wear away, Earth's surface to create other kinds of super lands. Over millions of years, for example, water flowing in the Colorado River carved the mile-deep Grand Canyon.

For Native American peoples, super lands are often very special places, and they have made up myths to explain how the features were formed. Today, many of North America's super lands are protected as national parks and monuments so that future generations may enjoy them.

HOW TO USE THIS BOOK

The 35 super lands in this book are arranged from west to east. Mexican super lands appear after those of the western states, and a Canadian one appears at the end. Each spread describes one landform. A map of North America locates it, and the "Field Notes" entry gives another fact about it. If you see a word you don't know, look it up in the Glossary on page 76.

KILAUEA

In the Hawaiian language, Kilauea means "much erupting." That is exactly what this very active volcano does. The lava that pours from Kilauea adds new land to the Big Island of Hawaii.

WHERE TO FIND:
Kilauea is located on the southeastern part of the Big Island of Hawaii in the Pacific Ocean.

WHAT TO LOOK FOR:

✳ WHAT IT IS
Kilauea is one of the world's most active volcanoes.

✳ SIZE
It rises 4,078 feet above sea level.

✳ HOW IT WAS FORMED
The volcano was created when melted rock from deep within the Earth erupted through cracks in the seafloor.

✳ MORE
Kilauea once erupted with a fountain of lava some 1,900 feet high.

Molten lava pours from the crater of Kilauea. Hawaiian tradition says that Pele, goddess of volcanic fires, lives there.

FIELD NOTES

The Hawaiian Islands formed over a spot on the floor of the Pacific where melted rock wells up.

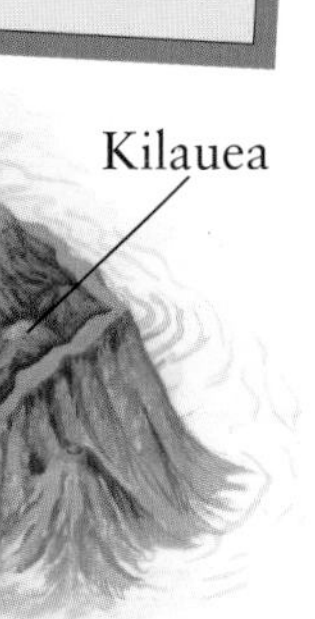

MOUNT McKINLEY

Rising high into the clouds, Mount McKinley often hides its snowy peak. When the weather is clear, the massive mountain towers over the landscape. Alaska natives call it Denali, which means "white one."

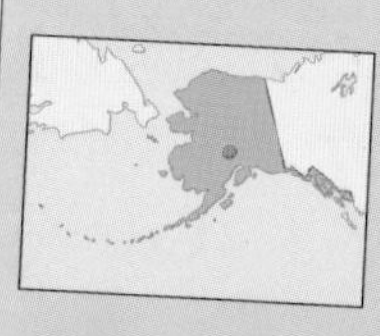

WHERE TO FIND:
Mount McKinley is part of the Alaska Range, mountains that rise in central Alaska.

WHAT TO LOOK FOR:

✳ WHAT IT IS
Mount McKinley is the highest mountain in North America.

✳ SIZE
It reaches 20,320 feet above sea level.

✳ HOW IT WAS FORMED
Land along a fault, a crack in the Earth's surface, rose when plates underneath it moved.

✳ MORE
McKinley has 17 major glaciers, 4 of them more than 25 miles long.

No trees can survive the cold on the slopes of Denali. Snow and ice in the form of glaciers cover them.

GLACIER BAY

A little more than 200 years ago, Glacier Bay didn't even exist. Glaciers, masses of slowly moving ice, up to 4,000 feet thick covered the area. The ice began to melt, uncovering land that became flooded by the sea.

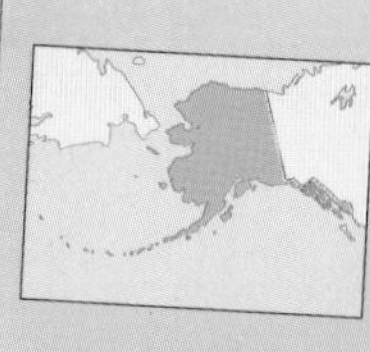

WHERE TO FIND:

Glacier Bay is located on the coast of southeastern Alaska, in an area known as the Panhandle.

WHAT TO LOOK FOR:

✳ WHAT IT IS
Glacier Bay is a bay formed by the fast retreat, or shrinking, of a glacier.

✳ SIZE
The bay, which branches into two parts, covers 5,125 square miles.

✳ HOW IT WAS FORMED
As the ice melted, it left a deep valley, which filled with seawater.

✳ MORE
The 65-mile retreat of the Glacier Bay ice is the fastest ever recorded.

FIELD NOTES

Chunks of ice up to 200 feet high break off, or calve, from glaciers and fall into the sea with a crash.

A total of 17 glaciers meet the sea at Glacier Bay.

CRATER LAKE

High in the mountains of western Oregon sits Crater Lake, deeper and bluer than any other lake in North America. Cliffs up to 2,000 feet high circle the clear and very pure water.

FIELD NOTES

Indian legend says the mountain bluebird was gray until it took a dip in the waters of Crater Lake.

Wizard Island, shaped like a sorcerer's hat, rises from Crater Lake. It formed from a cone of volcanic ash.

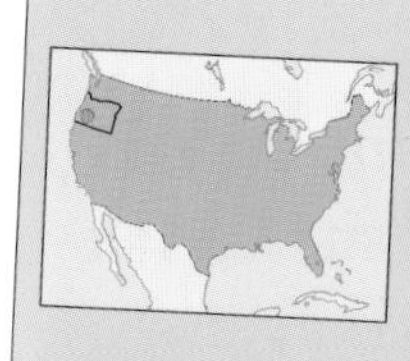

WHERE TO FIND:

Crater Lake is found high in the Cascades, a volcanic mountain range in western Oregon.

WHAT TO LOOK FOR:

✱ WHAT IT IS

At 1,900 feet deep, Crater Lake is the deepest lake in the United States.

✱ SIZE

Crater Lake covers 21 square miles.

✱ HOW IT WAS FORMED

The lake bed was created when the summit of an ancient volcano collapsed after an eruption.

✱ MORE

Snow, rain, and springwater fill the lake. It is so deep it rarely freezes over.

OREGON SEA STACKS

These rock pillars rise like watchmen in the ocean. Some look like stranded animals. Others are arches and bridges that lead to nowhere. Sea stacks were once attached to land.

FIELD NOTES

In the past, ships often crashed into sea stacks and were wrecked, especially at night or in bad weather.

Sunset silhouettes sea stacks off the Oregon coast at Cannon Beach.

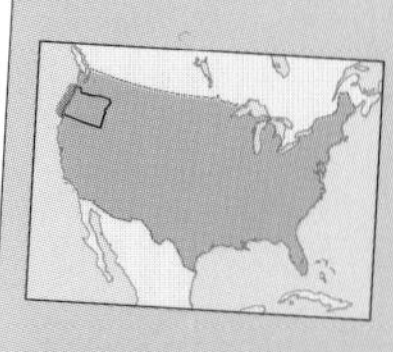

WHERE TO FIND:
These sea stacks lie off the coast of Oregon. Stacks are found off many coastlines throughout the world.

WHAT TO LOOK FOR:

✷ WHAT IT IS
Sea stacks are large rock pillars that occur off coastlines.

✷ SIZE
They range greatly in size from a few feet high to more than a hundred feet.

✷ HOW IT WAS FORMED
Weathering and erosion cut off sea stacks from the mainland.

✷ MORE
Wind and water may wear away a hole in a stack that develops into an arch.

SAN ANDREAS FAULT

From the air people can see a large gash on the land along the California coast. This break in the Earth's crust occurs where two plates that make up Earth's crust meet.

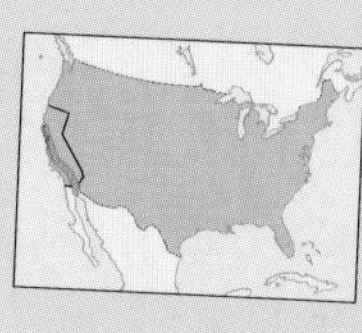

WHERE TO FIND:
The San Andreas Fault occurs about 50 miles inland along the coast of California.

WHAT TO LOOK FOR:

✱ WHAT IT IS
The San Andreas is a fault, or fracture, where rock moves sideways.

✱ SIZE
It runs about 700 miles, north to south.

✱ HOW IT WAS FORMED
The fault formed from movement at the boundary of two of the plates that make up Earth's crust.

✱ MORE
Geologists think a big earthquake will occur there in the next 20 years.

FIELD NOTES

In ten million years, Los Angeles will travel north 300 miles with its plate and will be west of San Francisco.

More than 10,000 earthquakes, most of them small, occur each year along the San Andreas Fault.

YOSEMITE VALLEY

Nature's wonders seem to meet in Yosemite. Granite domes and walls soar above the valley. Ribbon-like waterfalls tumble from cliffs, and colorful wildflowers blanket the meadows.

WHERE TO FIND:
The Yosemite Valley is located in the Sierra Nevada mountain range of central California.

WHAT TO LOOK FOR:

✱ WHAT IT IS
The Yosemite Valley is one of the world's most spectacular examples of the action of glaciers.

✱ SIZE
It is a mile wide and seven miles long.

✱ HOW IT WAS FORMED
Glacial ice widened, shaped, and smoothed the valley of the Merced River.

✱ MORE
Three of the world's highest waterfalls are found here.

FIELD NOTES

Yosemite Falls, the highest waterfall in North America at 2,425 feet, is the world's second highest falls.

Glaciers scraped off one side of a massive granite block, leaving a rounded top known as Half Dome.

DEATH VALLEY

Named for gold-seeking miners who died trying to cross it in 1849, Death Valley is North America's, lowest, driest, and hottest place. The continent's warmest air temperature was recorded there: 134°F.

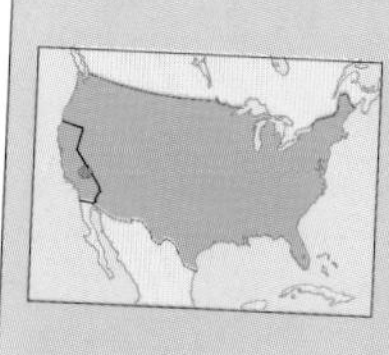

WHERE TO FIND:

Death Valley is located in the corner of southeastern California along the border with Nevada.

WHAT TO LOOK FOR:

✱ WHAT IT IS
Death Valley is a desert basin that lies between two mountain ranges.

✱ SIZE
It is 140 miles long and 5 to 15 miles wide.

✱ HOW IT WAS FORMED
Movement along a fault in the Earth's crust caused a basin, or depression, to form on the surface.

✱ MORE
The valley sits 282 feet below sea level.

Rippling sand dunes are a major feature of Death Valley, which receives only 1½ inches of rain a year.

FIELD NOTES

In the 1900s, miners dug borax, a mineral used for cleaning. It was hauled out of the valley by mules.

HELLS CANYON

According to Indian legend, a god in the form of a coyote created incredibly steep Hells Canyon to keep giants away from a local village. At the bottom of the canyon runs the Snake River.

At its widest point, Hells Canyon measures nine miles across.

WHERE TO FIND:

Hells Canyon is located along the border between Oregon and Idaho in the Northwest.

WHAT TO LOOK FOR:

✱ WHAT IT IS
Hells Canyon is the deepest gorge in North America.

✱ SIZE
Hells Canyon gorge plunges 7,900 feet—about 1½ miles.

✱ HOW IT WAS FORMED
The Snake River carved through an ancient mountain range.

✱ MORE
The canyon could hold six Empire State Buildings stacked on top of each other.

FIELD NOTES

Canyon rafters on the Snake River ride white water on some of the wildest rapids in North America.

GREAT SALT LAKE

If you've ever swallowed a mouthful of seawater, you know how salty it can be. Imagine a lake eight times saltier than the ocean! That's the Great Salt Lake.

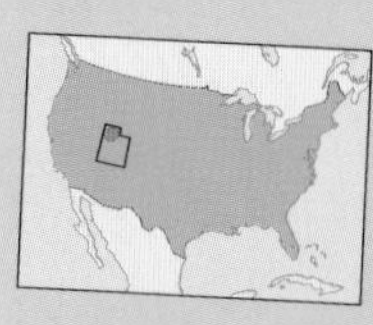

WHERE TO FIND:

The Great Salt Lake is located just outside Salt Lake City, in northwestern Utah.

WHAT TO LOOK FOR:

✱ WHAT IT IS
It is a huge, salty lake.

✱ SIZE
The Great Salt Lake is about 75 miles long and 30 to 50 miles wide.

✱ HOW IT WAS FORMED
It is the remains of Lake Bonneville, an ancient inland lake that once covered much of the region.

✱ MORE
Its size and salt content vary depending on the amount of rainfall.

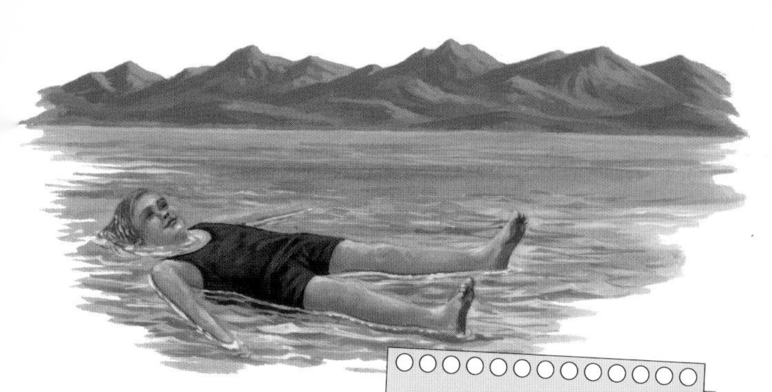

FIELD NOTES

There is so much salt in the Great Salt Lake that people can float in the water very easily.

Antelope, more than 15 miles in length, is the biggest of three large islands that dot the southern portion of the Great Salt Lake.

BRYCE CANYON

Some rocks look like church spires, one like an alligator, another like a sinking ship. Bryce is not one canyon but many, cut by streams that flow only after big rainstorms.

Paiute Indian legend says Bryce's stone pillars are part-human animals turned to stone for bad deeds.

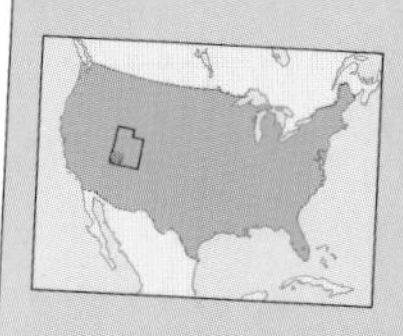

WHERE TO FIND:

Bryce Canyon is a feature of the Paunsaugunt (pawn-SAW-gunt) Plateau region of southwestern Utah.

WHAT TO LOOK FOR:

✱ WHAT IT IS

Bryce is a series of canyons carved from the eastern edge of a high plateau.

✱ SIZE

Bryce covers 35,835 acres.

✱ HOW IT WAS FORMED

The shapes formed from water freezing and thawing in the cracks of rock, wearing it away.

✱ MORE

Melting snows and heavy summer rains also help shape the rock formations.

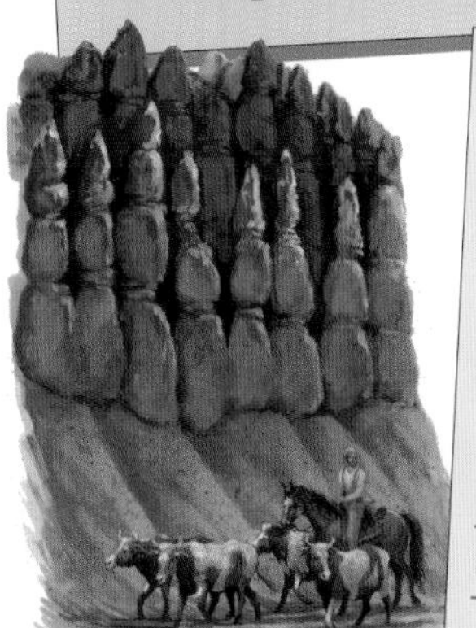

FIELD NOTES

Mormon farmers settling near here in the 19th century tried to graze cattle among the maze-like rocks.

ARCHES NATIONAL PARK

Like giant doorways, sandstone arches dot the desert. They were once part of thick layers of rock. Over time, weather carved arches in the layers.

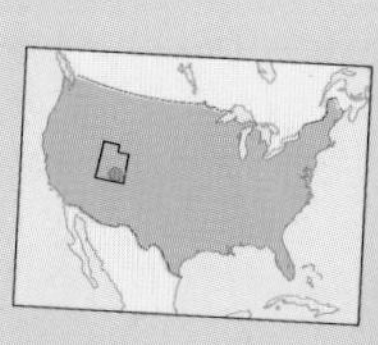

WHERE TO FIND:

Arches National Park is located in the Colorado Plateau region of eastern Utah.

WHAT TO LOOK FOR:

✱ WHAT IT IS
Arches contains more than 950 natural openings in sandstone rock.

✱ SIZE
The arches range from 3 to 306 feet wide and are up to 106 feet high.

✱ HOW IT WAS FORMED
Wind and water widened cracks in rock, then shaped it into arches.

✱ MORE
Over time, wind and water continue to weather arches, and they collapse.

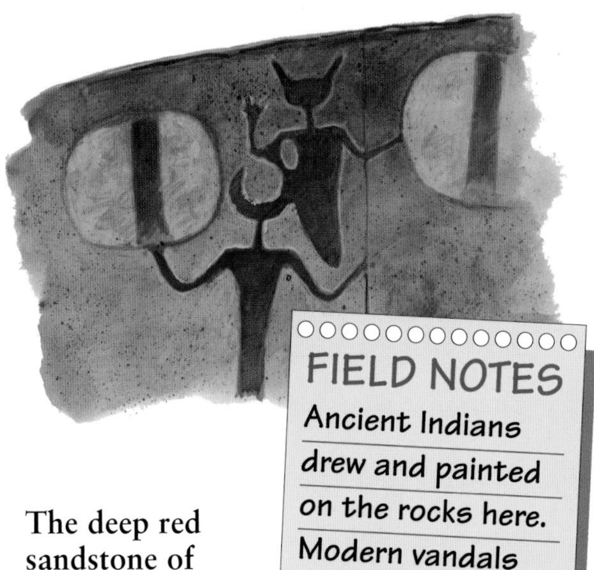

FIELD NOTES

Ancient Indians drew and painted on the rocks here. Modern vandals have destroyed some of this art.

The deep red sandstone of Delicate Arch frames the high mountains beyond it.

GRAND CANYON

Standing on the edge of the Grand Canyon, you can see far into the past. Exposed rock near the bottom dates back 1.7 billion years! The canyon is so big it takes five hours to drive around it from rim to rim.

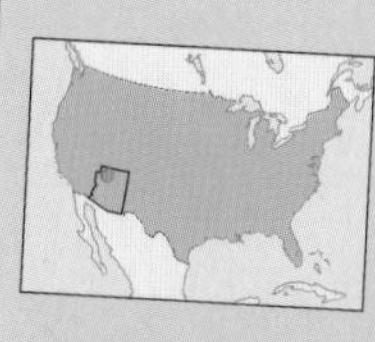

WHERE TO FIND:
The Grand Canyon is found along the Colorado River on the Colorado Plateau in northern Arizona.

WHAT TO LOOK FOR:

✱ WHAT IT IS
The Grand Canyon is the world's largest gorge.

✱ SIZE
It is 290 miles long, up to 18 miles wide, and about 1 mile deep.

✱ HOW IT WAS FORMED
The Colorado River cut through layers of many different kinds of rock.

✱ MORE
On a clear day, you can see 200 miles from the canyon's rim.

After a 1903 visit, President Theodore Roosevelt called it "the one great site every American... should see."

FIELD NOTES

In the 1800s, one-armed Maj. John Wesley Powell made two expeditions to explore and map the Grand Canyon.

PETRIFIED FOREST

Dinosaurs once roamed lush marshes here. Now, the Petrified Forest is a desert littered with preserved remains, or fossils, of trees, other plants, and animals. The fossils have petrified, or turned to stone.

Chunks of fossilized logs appear in clusters throughout the Petrified Forest.

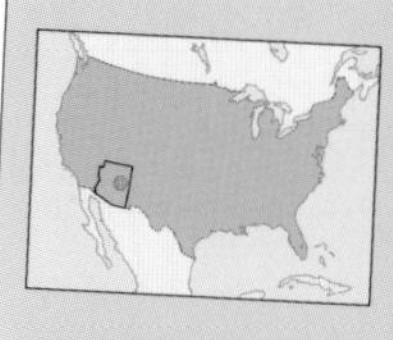

WHERE TO FIND:

The Petrified Forest is a national park located in the larger Painted Desert area of east-central Arizona.

WHAT TO LOOK FOR:

✱ WHAT IT IS
Petrified Forest is probably the world's largest concentration of petrified logs.

✱ SIZE
Some logs are up to 170 feet long, and one is 9½ feet in diameter.

✱ HOW IT WAS FORMED
Minerals in water replaced the wood tissue of trees buried in an ancient flood.

✱ MORE
It is illegal for visitors to take away pieces of the petrified wood.

FIELD NOTES

The many colors of quartz, one of the minerals in the fossil, gleam in a polished slab of petrified log.

OLD FAITHFUL

Every day, thousands of visitors to Yellowstone National Park wait for this geyser, a hot spring that jets hot water and steam, to erupt. It seldom disappoints them, erupting about every 75 to 79 minutes.

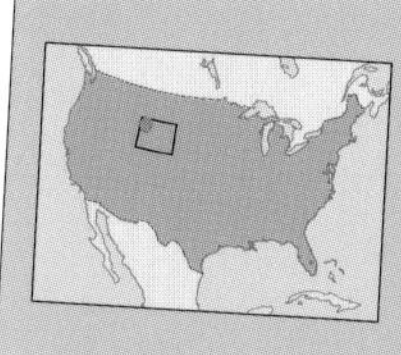

WHERE TO FIND:

Old Faithful is located in Yellowstone National Park, on the borders of Wyoming, Idaho, and Montana.

WHAT TO LOOK FOR:

✳ WHAT IT IS
Old Faithful is the world's most predictable geyser.

✳ SIZE
It spouts a column of water and steam up to 200 feet high.

✳ HOW IT WAS FORMED
Deep, molten rock boils water that shoots up through a narrow space.

✳ MORE
It is one of 10,000 features in the park created by heat inside the Earth.

FIELD NOTES

Along with Old Faithful, Mammoth Hot Springs is one of many wonders in Yellowstone park.

On a bright, breezy day, the wind blows Old Faithful's column of water and steam sideways.

DEVILS TOWER

Devils Tower juts skyward from the flat, high plains of northeastern Wyoming. For more than a hundred years, people have climbed to its summit.

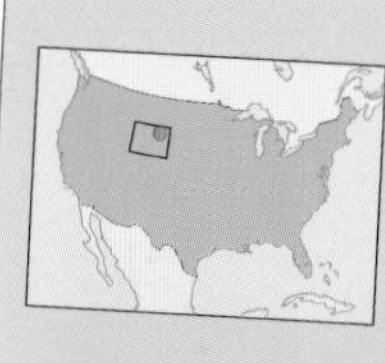

WHERE TO FIND:

Devils Tower is located along the Belle Fourche River in the Black Hills area of Wyoming.

WHAT TO LOOK FOR:

✷ WHAT IT IS
Devils Tower is a column of molten rock that hardened.

✷ SIZE
It is 865 feet high.

✷ HOW IT WAS FORMED
Lava filled the core of an ancient volcano. Over time, all of the volcano but the tower weathered away.

✷ MORE
The Kiowa Indians called the tower Bear Lodge.

FIELD NOTES

In Kiowa legend the tower was a tree stump that rose when seven girls climbed atop it to escape a bear.

The Kiowa believed that the tower's ridges were claw marks made by the bear in the legend.

GREAT SAND DUNES

Like an out-of-place desert, enormous sand dunes lie at the base of the Sangre de Cristo Range, part of the Rocky Mountains. Some of the dunes are more than 700 feet high.

Strong winds change the size and shape of the Great Sand Dunes constantly.

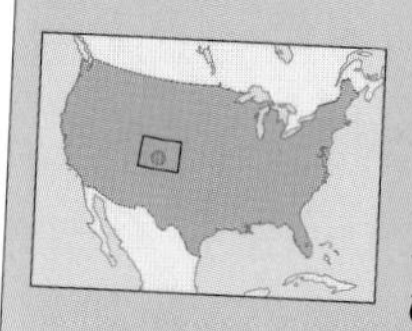

WHERE TO FIND:

The Great Sand Dunes are located in the Rocky Mountains of south-central Colorado.

WHAT TO LOOK FOR:

✱ WHAT IT IS
It is a huge field of dunes taller than any others in the United States.

✱ SIZE
The dunes cover 39 square miles.

✱ HOW IT WAS FORMED
Rocks of the surrounding mountains weathered into sand grains. The wind then blew the sand into dunes.

✱ MORE
A creek at the edge of the dunes forms a beach area.

FIELD NOTES

No plants grow on the Great Sand Dunes. People can climb on and slide down them without causing harm.

SHIP ROCK

On a hot, hazy day, Ship Rock shimmers on the dry New Mexico plain. Early white settlers thought it looked like an old-fashioned sailing ship.

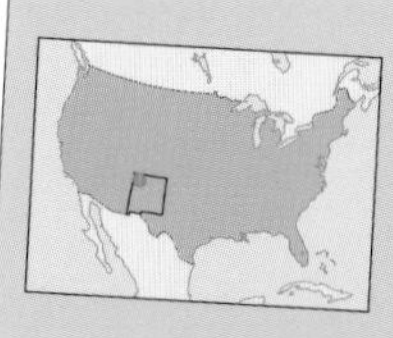

WHERE TO FIND:

Ship Rock lies in the Four Corners area of New Mexico, on land belonging to the Navajo Indians.

WHAT TO LOOK FOR:

*** WHAT IT IS**
Ship Rock is a monolith, the name for a single great mass of rock.

*** SIZE**
It is 1,700 feet high.

*** HOW IT WAS FORMED**
It formed when melted rock filled the neck of a volcano and hardened. The rest of the volcano has since eroded.

*** MORE**
The Navajo name for Ship Rock means "the winged rock."

Because Ship Rock is sacred to the Navajo, climbing it is forbidden.

FIELD NOTES

For centuries, Ship Rock has been a sign to the Navajo that they have entered their sacred homeland.

CARLSBAD CAVERNS

The desert above Carlsbad Caverns gives no hint of what lies below. Water in the ground dissolved limestone rock, carving more than 80 caves.

Drop by drop, limestone dissolved in water built Carlsbad's features, such as these towering stalagmites.

FIELD NOTES

Every evening a million Mexican free-tailed bats swoop out of Carlsbad to hunt insects to eat.

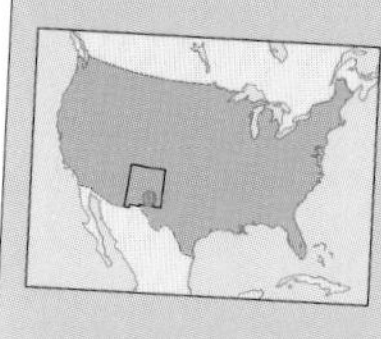

WHERE TO FIND:
The caverns are located in the Guadalupe Mountains of southeastern New Mexico.

WHAT TO LOOK FOR:

✱ WHAT IT IS
Carlsbad has one of the deepest, largest, and most decorated caverns in the world.

✱ SIZE
The cave system covers 46,766 acres.

✱ HOW IT WAS FORMED
Water dissolved limestone left by an ancient inland sea.

✱ MORE
Carlsbad has been called "the Grand Canyon with a roof on it."

COPPER CANYON

The Tarahumara, local Indians, say that Copper Canyon is "halfway to heaven." For centuries they have lived and farmed on the flatter areas of their mountain canyon home.

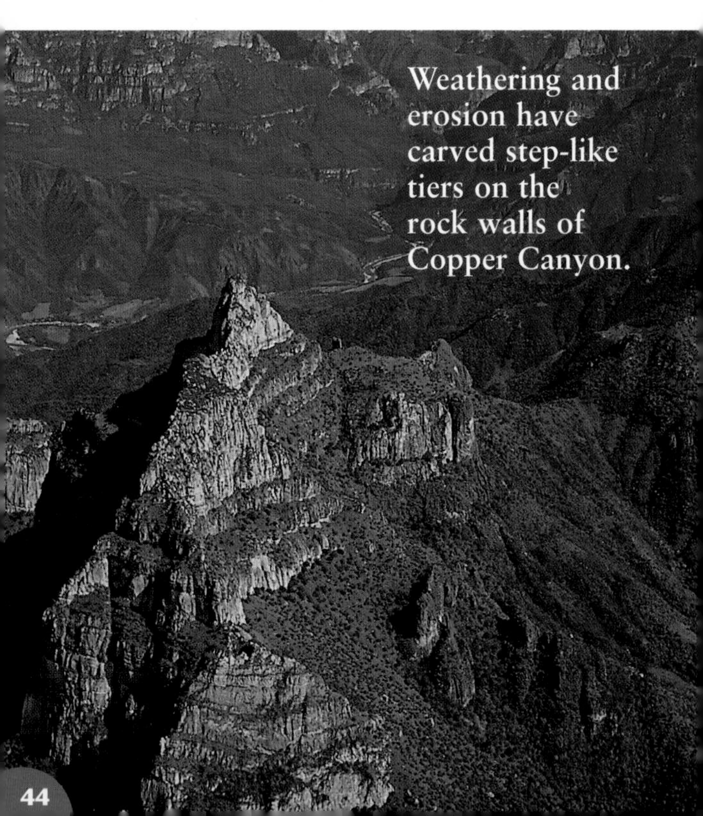

Weathering and erosion have carved step-like tiers on the rock walls of Copper Canyon.

WHERE TO FIND:

Copper Canyon is located in the Tarahumara Mountain range of western Mexico.

WHAT TO LOOK FOR:

✷ WHAT IT IS
Copper Canyon is actually a series of rugged canyons.

✷ SIZE
Peaks at Copper Canyon reach more than 8,000 feet high, and some canyons are 6,000 feet deep.

✷ HOW IT WAS FORMED
Rivers and streams cut the canyons.

✷ MORE
Miners once dug silver, gold, copper, lead, and zinc from Copper Canyon.

FIELD NOTES

The Tarahumara use mules to travel narrow paths on the steep slopes of Copper Canyon.

CHICHÉN ITZÁ CENOTE

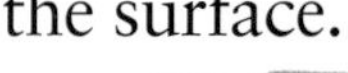

The Maya Indians of Mexico had to plan their settlements near cenotes (sih-NO-teez), or natural wells. The area's limestone rock absorbs water here, and it sinks below the surface.

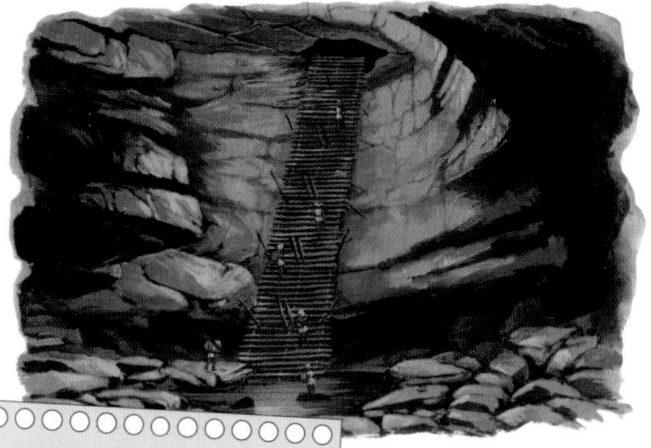

FIELD NOTES

The Maya built ladders in some cenotes. At times they threw human sacrifices into the natural wells.

People have not used the cenote at Chichén Itzá for many centuries. It is now overgrown with plants.

WHERE TO FIND:

Chichén Itzá is located in the central part of the Yucatán Peninsula, in eastern Mexico.

WHAT TO LOOK FOR:

✱ WHAT IT IS
A cenote is a natural limestone well.

✱ SIZE
The Chichén Itzá cenote is about 200 feet in diameter.

✱ HOW IT WAS FORMED
Cenotes form in areas where water sinks into porous rock and collects in hollow places called sinkholes.

✱ MORE
The Maya called the cenote at Chichén Itzá the Sacred Well.

BADLANDS

If you drive through the southern plains of South Dakota, you might think you've landed on the moon. From the flat land, a wall of rock suddenly rises. It is sculpted into fantastic ridges, peaks, and gullies.

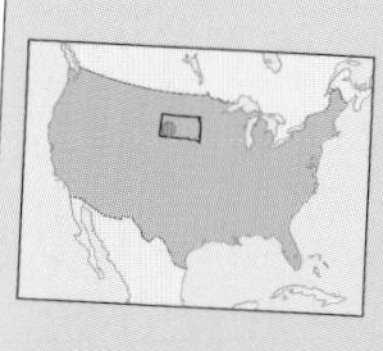

WHERE TO FIND:

The Badlands area is located in southwestern South Dakota. Much of it is a national park.

WHAT TO LOOK FOR:

✱ WHAT IT IS
The Badlands is an immense wall of weathered rock.

✱ SIZE
It stretches for a hundred miles.

✱ HOW IT WAS FORMED
Water, wind, and frost carved layers of rock formed from the deposits of ancient rivers.

✱ MORE
Badlands rock contains many fossil plants and animals.

French fur trappers named it the Badlands because it had "bad lands to travel across."

FIELD NOTES

In 1890, Chief Bigfoot of the Ogalala Sioux led his people through the pass now named for him.

BLACK HILLS

From a distance, the Black Hills do look black, due to the dark ponderosa pine trees that cover them. Gold in the area brought prospectors here in the 19th century.

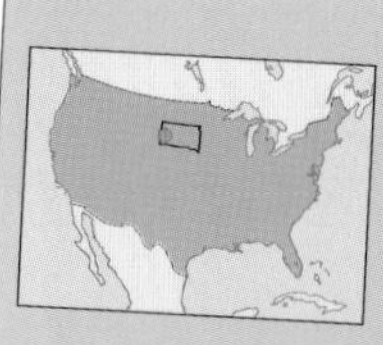

WHERE TO FIND:

The Black Hills are located in an area of plains on the border of Wyoming and South Dakota.

WHAT TO LOOK FOR:

✱ WHAT IT IS
It is a region of forested hills.

✱ SIZE
The Black Hills area covers about 1,875 square miles.

✱ HOW IT WAS FORMED
Volcanic activity within the Earth thrust up a bulge of molten rock that formed low mountains on the plains.

✱ MORE
Herds of bison roam here in a preserve, an area that is protected by law.

Some of the rocks in the Black Hills are among the oldest in North America. They formed 2.5 billion years ago.

FIELD NOTES

Sculptor Gutzon Borglum carved the faces of four Presidents on Mount Rushmore, in the Black Hills.

CHIMNEY ROCK

Pioneers in covered wagons traveling westward along the Oregon Trail used to rejoice at the site of Chimney Rock. It meant that one third of their long journey was over.

Some early travelers thought the sandstone spire looked like the chimney of a factory.

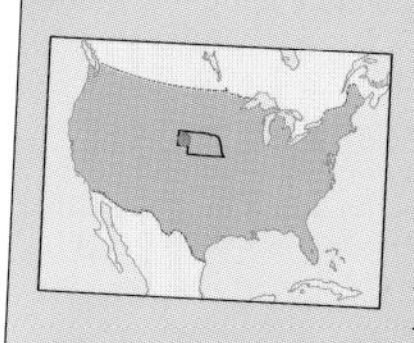

WHERE TO FIND:

Chimney Rock is located along the North Platte River in the plains area of western Nebraska.

WHAT TO LOOK FOR:

✱ WHAT IT IS
Chimney Rock is a sandstone pillar made of sand and other material that was part of the floor of an ancient sea.

✱ SIZE
It stands about 500 feet tall.

✱ HOW IT WAS FORMED
Weathering and erosion wore away the rest of the rock of the ancient seabed.

✱ MORE
Chimney Rock stands alone, the only monolith on the Nebraska plain.

FIELD NOTES

On clear days, westward-bound wagon trains could see Chimney Rock from as far away as 30 miles.

BOUNDARY WATERS CANOE AREA

Up in the North Woods lies one of the continent's most spectacular wildernesses. Hundreds of lakes and rivers offer miles and miles of canoe routes.

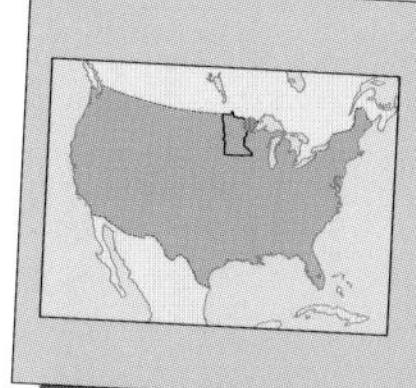

WHERE TO FIND:

Boundary Waters is located on the border between northeastern Minnesota and Ontario, Canada.

WHAT TO LOOK FOR:

✱ WHAT IT IS
Boundary Waters is an immense area filled with lakes and rivers.

✱ SIZE
It covers more than two million acres.

✱ HOW IT WAS FORMED
Glaciers carved the land and waterways here.

✱ MORE
Many lakes are connected by portages, trails for carrying canoes from one place to another.

Canoeists paddle on a clear, island-dotted lake, part of some 1,200 miles of canoe routes in Boundary Waters.

FIELD NOTES

French fur traders, called voyageurs, traveled through Boundary Waters in the 18th and 19th centuries.

MISSISSIPPI RIVER

There is no greater river in the United States, or in all of North America. Together with the Missouri River, which feeds into it, the Mississippi forms the continent's most important river system.

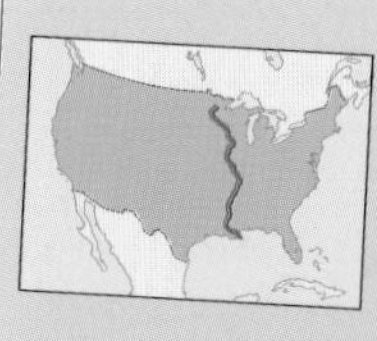

WHERE TO FIND:

The drainage area of the Mississippi-Missouri river system covers all or part of 31 states.

WHAT TO LOOK FOR:

✱ WHAT IT IS
The Mississippi-Missouri is the longest river in the United States.

✱ SIZE
The river system is 3,708 miles long.

✱ HOW IT WAS FORMED
The Mississippi River rises from Lake Itasca in northern Minnesota.

✱ MORE
The name Mississippi means "father of waters" in the Algonkian Indian language.

Flat-bottomed boats called barges carry many kinds of goods up and down the Mississippi.

FIELD NOTES

From Lake Itasca, the Mississippi River flows south all the way to Louisiana and the Gulf of Mexico.

LOUISIANA BAYOU

Shallow waters, lush with tall, moss-draped trees and alive with frogs croaking and catfish biting—these are the sights and sounds of a Louisiana bayou. Wildlife thrives there.

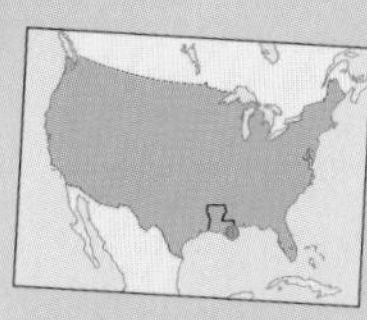

WHERE TO FIND:
Bayous are common in the southern United States, especially along the Gulf Coast and the Mississippi.

WHAT TO LOOK FOR:

*** WHAT IT IS**
A bayou is a marshy creek or a swampy backwater of a river or lake.

*** SIZE**
Bayous cover more than one-fourth of Louisiana.

*** HOW IT WAS FORMED**
Bayous form in low, flat areas where water can collect.

*** MORE**
French-Canadian people called Cajuns settled in the Louisiana bayous.

FIELD NOTES
The pirate Jean Lafitte, when not attacking ships in the Gulf of Mexico, often hid out in Louisiana bayous.

A white swamp lily grows among marsh grasses in the slow-moving waters of a bayou in southern Louisiana.

FLORIDA KEYS

A long string of islands curls off Florida's tip. Called the Florida Keys—a key is a low island—they keep the rough surf of the Atlantic Ocean away from Florida Bay.

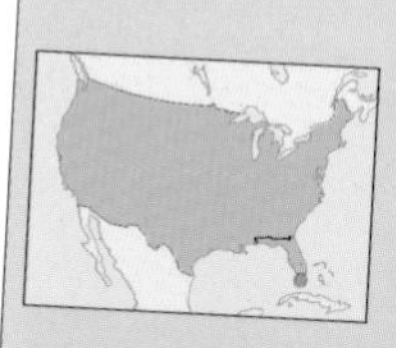

WHERE TO FIND:
The Florida Keys are located off southern Florida. They stretch from Key Biscayne to Key West.

WHAT TO LOOK FOR:

✱ **WHAT IT IS**
The Florida Keys are barrier islands, islands that protect the shore from the effects of the ocean.

✱ **SIZE**
The keys stretch for 150 miles.

✱ **HOW IT WAS FORMED**
The keys built up from limestone and from remains of an ancient coral reef.

✱ **MORE**
They shelter many endangered species, including tiny Key deer.

Colorful fish swim along a coral reef in Key Biscayne, part of the northernmost reef in the U.S. that is still growing.

FIELD NOTES

Tiny creatures called polyps build stony skeletons as they grow. Over time, the skeletons form a coral reef.

EVERGLADES

The Everglades is a natural community, or ecosystem, unlike any other. Water inches deep supports marsh grasses, mangrove trees, and other plants near the Florida coast.

FIELD NOTES

Florida panthers usually hide in the dense plant life of the Everglades. Few of these big cats are left.

In this watery realm live more than 300 species of birds and many other kinds of wildlife.

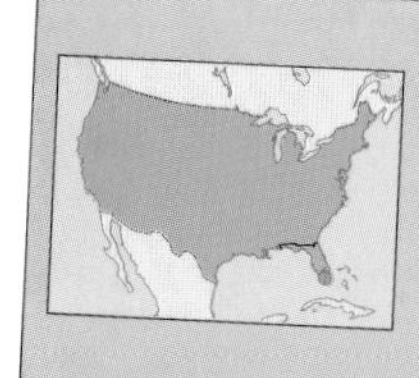

WHERE TO FIND:

The Everglades is located on the southern tip of Florida and extends from Lake Okeechobee to Florida Bay.

WHAT TO LOOK FOR:

*** WHAT IT IS**
The Everglades is a slowly moving sheet of water. A national park covers much of the area.

*** SIZE**
It is 50 miles wide and 100 miles long.

*** HOW IT WAS FORMED**
Water spilling from Lake Okeechobee slowly travels south to Florida Bay.

*** MORE**
Local Indians called the area Pa-hay-okee, meaning "the grassy waters."

OKEFENOKEE SWAMP

If you were looking for a spooky swamp as a setting for a mystery, Okefenokee would be a great choice. Little has changed in this watery wilderness for thousands of years.

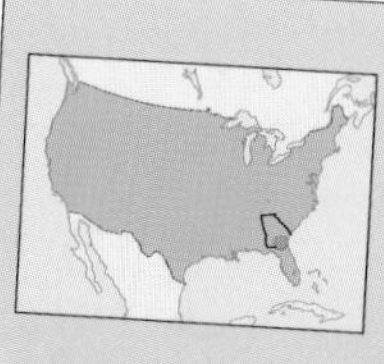

WHERE TO FIND:

The Okefenokee Swamp lies on the border between northeastern Florida and southeastern Georgia.

WHAT TO LOOK FOR:

✳ WHAT IT IS
It is a large swamp containing cypress and pine trees, peat bogs, and grasses.

✳ SIZE
It covers more than 600 square miles.

✳ HOW IT WAS FORMED
Water from rain and streams filled a depression that was once part of the ocean floor.

✳ MORE
Okefenokee means "black waters" in the language of local Indians.

FIELD NOTES

Protected by law, alligators thrive in the Okefenokee. Plants stain the waters of the swamp dark.

Cypress trees send long roots into the murky waters of Okefenokee Swamp. If scraped by a passing boat, the roots make a creaking sound.

MAMMOTH CAVE

Beneath the wooded Kentucky hills, emerald green rivers run deep. They carve a maze of passageways miles long, huge chambers, and tall shafts. The waters shape five levels of caves.

WHERE TO FIND:

Mammoth Cave, a national park, is located in the wooded hill region of south-central Kentucky.

WHAT TO LOOK FOR:

✱ WHAT IT IS
Mammoth Cave is the longest known cave system in the world.

✱ SIZE
The caverns extend about 360 miles.

✱ HOW IT WAS FORMED
Ancient underground rivers dissolved limestone to make tunnel-like cave passages.

✱ MORE
Tourists came after a settler discovered the cave while tracking a wounded bear.

At Mammoth Cave, long passageways lead to large chambers decorated with natural sculptures.

FIELD NOTES

These eyeless fish are among many blind and colorless animals that live in Mammoth's dark world.

NATURAL BRIDGE

Future President Thomas Jefferson bought Natural Bridge from King George III while the Colonies belonged to England. The bridge was sacred to local Indians.

A local story says that Monacan Indians found the bridge while being chased by nearby tribes.

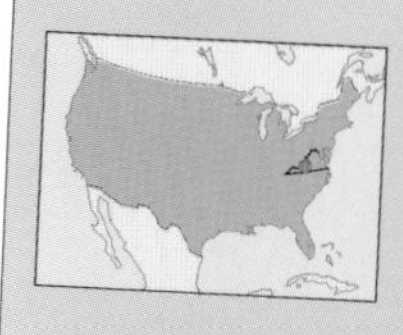

WHERE TO FIND:

Natural Bridge is located in the Appalachian Mountains of southwestern Virginia, in the canyon of a creek.

WHAT TO LOOK FOR:

✳WHAT IT IS
Natural Bridge is a naturally formed rock bridge.

✳SIZE
It is 200 feet high and 90 feet long. It spans 150 feet at its widest point.

✳HOW IT WAS FORMED
A creek cut through soft rock over thousands of years.

✳MORE
Colonists dropped molten lead from it to make bullets.

FIELD NOTES

Thomas Jefferson visited the bridge on horseback and planned lodgings there to attract visitors.

ASSATEAGUE ISLAND

Assateague is never the same from day to day. The Atlantic Ocean changes its shape by moving sand from one place to another. When storms hit, waves can create big changes.

FIELD NOTES

Ponies, perhaps descendants of shipwrecked horses, feed on the island's salty grasses.

Ocean surf moves sand, adding on to the southwestern end of Assateague.

WHERE TO FIND:

Assateague Island borders the Atlantic Ocean off the coasts of Maryland and Virginia.

WHAT TO LOOK FOR:

* WHAT IT IS

Assateague is a barrier island.

* SIZE

It is 37 miles long and up to 2 miles wide.

* HOW IT WAS FORMED

Over time, fierce storms drove the sea to break through beach dunes, eventually forming islands.

* MORE

Assateague is home to some 200 species of birds.

MOUNT WASHINGTON

You may think the strongest winds in the world blew at the North Pole. Guess again. They occurred on the summit of New Hampshire's Mount Washington.

FIELD NOTES

An anemometer (ah-nuh-MA-muh-tur) measured a wind speed here of 231 miles an hour in 1934.

Many kinds of weather data—about storms, clouds, and fog—are collected at an observatory on Mount Washington.

WHERE TO FIND:

Mount Washington lies in the White Mountains, a range of the Appalachians, in eastern New Hampshire.

WHAT TO LOOK FOR:

✱ WHAT IT IS
Mount Washington is the tallest mountain in the Northeast.

✱ SIZE
It rises 6,288 feet.

✱ HOW IT WAS FORMED
It is in a mountain range pushed up when two plates of Earth's crust collided.

✱ MORE
Scientists conduct important weather research here, such as the study of how ice forms on airplanes.

NIAGARA FALLS

With a sound like thunder, the Niagara River tumbles over steep cliffs. About six million gallons of water—enough to fill 20,000 bathtubs—rushes over the rocky rim every minute.

WHERE TO FIND:
Niagara Falls lies on the Niagara River on the border between Ontario, Canada, and New York State.

WHAT TO LOOK FOR:

✶ WHAT IT IS
It includes two separate falls and is the largest waterfall in North America.

✶ SIZE
The Canadian Falls is a half mile wide; the American is a thousand feet wide.

✶ HOW IT WAS FORMED
Niagara Falls formed some 10,000 years ago when water from melting glaciers created the Niagara River.

✶ MORE
The Canadian Falls is horseshoe shaped.

FIELD NOTES

Visitors in rain slickers climb down stairs to get a close-up look at the American Falls.

Waters rushing over the edge of the falls wear away about one inch of rock every year.

GLOSSARY

canyon A deep valley with steep sides, often with a river running through it.

continent One of the seven major divisions of land on Earth: Asia, Africa, North America, South America, Antarctica, Europe, and Australia.

crater A bowl-shaped depression made by a volcanic eruption or a meteorite.

crust The rocky, outermost layer of the Earth.

ecosystem One of the Earth's natural communities in which living and nonliving things coexist in their environment.

erosion The movement of material that has been loosened by weathering from one place to another. Water, ice, wind, and gravity cause the movement.

fault A break in the Earth's crust along which great masses of rock move.

geyser A hot spring from which jets of water and stream erupt.

glacier A mass of ice that moves slowly over land.

gorge A deep and narrow valley with very steep sides.

plate One of many huge rocky slabs that make up the outer shell of the Earth.

plateau A large flat area that is higher than the surrounding land.

stalagmite A deposit on the floor of a cave formed over time by the dripping of water that contains minerals.

weathering The breaking down of rocks by water, ice, acid, plants, and changes in temperature.

INDEX OF **SUPER LANDS**

ABOUT THE CONSULTANTS

Peter B. Stifel is an associate professor emeritus at the University of Maryland, College Park. His 30 years of teaching involved physical and historical geology; vertebrate, invertebrate, and micropaleontology; biostratigraphy; and evolution. He is corporation member and former trustee of the Sea Education Association of Woods Hole, Massachusetts, and serves on the Advisory Council of Cornell University's Shoals Marine Laboratory. He is a past president of the Geological Society of Washington and the Paleontological Society of Washington.

PHOTOGRAPHIC CREDITS

front cover David Muench **back cover** Joe McDonald/Earth Scenes **half title page** George Mobley **title page** Chris Johns **5** Marc Moritsch **7** James Amos **9** John Eastcott & Yva Momatiuk **11** Steve Raymer **13** Ray Gehman **15** Phil Schermeister **17** Phil Degginger/Earth Scenes **19** Marc Moritsch **20** Allstock/Phil Schofield **23** James Amos **24** David Alan Harvey **27** George Mobley **29** Randy Olson **31** Walter Edwards **32** Joe McDonald/Earth Scenes **35** Ray Gehman **37** Randy Olson **38** Walter Edwards **41** Phil Degginger/Earth Scenes **42** David Boyer **44** Phil Schermeister **47** Dani/Jeske/Earth Scenes **49** Stephen & Sylvia Sharnoff **51** John Lemker/Earth Scenes **52** Phil Schermeister **55** Ray Gehman **57** Allen Blake Sheldon **59** James P. Blair **61** James Amos **63** Medford Taylor **65** Brian Miller/Earth Scenes **67** Breck P. Kent/Earth Scenes **68** Richard Nowitz **71** Al Petteway **73** Dick Durrance **75** Sam Abell **77** George Mobley **79** Steve Raymer